DEANA SHARES

GEMS FROM THE HEART

By Deana Drake

Edited, Formatted, Designed & Published by

Wade Christian Publishing LLC

www.wadepublishers.com

info@wadepublishers.com

Deana Shares: Gems From the Heart

Written by Deana Drake

Paperback ISBN: 979-8-9857363-8-0

E-Book ISBN: 979-8-9857363-9-7

Dedication

This book is dedicated to my mom, one of the strongest women I know. She dealt with sickness my whole life, but she never gave up on anything that she set out to do.

I also dedicate this book to my mentor J. Michele. Although I was raised in church, she came into my life when I was seventeen and taught me what a true relationship with God was all about.

I would not be half the woman I am today without their love, teaching, and discipline. Until we meet again, I'll continue living life and sharing gems 💎.

Table of Contents

4

Deana Shares: Gems From the Heart was birthed from a place of pain that God would eventually reveal had a purpose. 2018 was one of my toughest seasons of life, but God performed spiritual surgery on my heart, and He wanted me to share my experiences to bless others. God revealed that He not only wanted me Healed but also made whole so another woman could see of His goodness.

I tasted true **Peace** and vowed to stay clear of confusion. I was content with being happy until I discovered **Joy**. I've hosted prayer calls, recorded podcast episodes, and started a YouTube channel to share my heart, and now God has blessed me with the opportunity to write a book. I pray that each one of my experiences will encourage you.

From my heart to yours,

Deana

What is My Purpose?

"I chose you before I formed you in the womb; I set you apart before you were born. I appointed you a prophet to the nations." - Jeremiah 1:5

God's will for you is to live out loud, purposefully, and unapologetically. He already chose you before placing you in your mother's womb to carry out His assignment on your life. Think about things that make you smile or bring you joy and there you will find your passion. For instance, a beautician is not just making money to support her family; she's called to help women look and feel good. I know when I feel good, I want to look good as well. Believe it or not, that beautician is called for a greater purpose, and what she carries another sister needs! I don't have the skills to do my own hair, but I'm blessed by the fruit of my beautician's hands (love me some Jessica). I've sat in the beauty salon for hours and had healthy conversations

about God, life, and family. Those conversations allowed me to
minister and be ministered to.

My purpose is to share the Word of God and encourage women from all walks of life. If you're reading this and don't know your purpose, I pray that God reveals it to you before the end of this book.

God Doesn't Play About You

"Do not touch My anointed ones or harm My prophets." - 1 Chronicles 16:22

Stop acting like you're not a big deal because you are, and God calls you the apple of His eye. Let's face it; He's crazy about you. It doesn't mean you're better than anyone else because He loves her just as much as He loves you, but I wrote this book for YOU, so take it personally.

God will not let anyone play with you if God doesn't play about you. "Do not touch My anointed or harm My prophets" is self-explanatory. The mature woman you are today will no longer allow mistreatment or disrespect. You are learning that everything doesn't require a response, and that battles are won on your knees!

It's very apparent that the hand of God is truly on your life, and even when they don't acknowledge it, you better believe they're watching.

Don't Be a Busy Body

To seek to lead a quiet life, to mind your own business, and to work with your own hands, as we commanded you, - 1 Thessalonians 4:11

There is a reason God blessed us with two ears and one mouth. He wants us to do more listening than we do talking. Over these last two years, God has really dealt with me about my mouth. If my words aren't building someone up, they could be tearing someone down! OUCH!

There's a slogan that says, "Mind the business that pays you," and that's real because we honestly don't have the time to be caught up in other people's affairs when we need to tend to our own. I went through a phase where I had to sit silently and gather my thoughts because God spoke to my heart about getting things in order. I had to denounce some things that were not of God spoken over me by others and words that I spoke over myself.

Turning my phone on Do Not Disturb was one of the best things I learned how to do, and I found out that I was more productive that way. I began to limit my time watching tv, stopped the ripping and running, and decreased my talking on the phone. It scared me at first because I realized how much I enjoyed not always having to be on every scene or spend so much time talking just to talk. God was teaching me how to quiet my spirit and make more time for Him by turning the noise of the world down and turning the things of God up.

Sister, learn to settle your spirit. Listen for those moments when God tells you to be quiet and when He tells you to speak. It's easy to be Martha in this busy world but be like Mary and take time to sit at his feet. Don't be busy being busy.

Authenticity

I will praise thee; for I am fearfully and wonderfully made: marvelous are thy works; and that my soul knoweth right well. – Psalm 139:14

I was in my late 30's when I began to feel the shifting and transformation that was taking place in my life. I fought for a long time to fit in but realized I was doing myself a disservice trying to live up to the expectations of others. It was draining and depressing. The best gift we can give someone is the gift of being ourselves. I'm goofy, sassy, genuine, sensitive, and loyal; yes, even with all my imperfections. God loves Him some me and you need to know that He loves Him some you as well.

Telling God that we desire to be someone other than who He made us is a smack in the face to Him. Of course, we don't say it verbally, but our actions tell it all. William Shakespeare said, "to thine own self be true." If I can't be true to myself, I can't be true to anyone else. I spent years trying to get others to like me and even tried to convince them to be my friend. However, God revealed that some people can't give you what they can't even offer themselves. WOW... that's deep! Being authentic is a blessing, and I pray that you give yourself the freedom, room, and permission to evolve into the best version of yourself because the world needs the real you. You GROW girl.

Forgiveness is For You

Then Jesus said, "Father forgive them because they do not know what they are doing." -Luke 23:34

Marianne Williamson said,
"Unforgiveness is like drinking poison yourself and waiting for the other person to die." Many children of God walk around with unresolved issues and unforgiveness in their hearts. I don't care what we think; we cannot truly worship God in freedom and truth this way. It's not saying what someone did to us didn't hurt, and yes they should be held accountable, but it must be dealt with when your peace is hindered.

The molestation wasn't your fault. Your daddy abandoning you hurt like hell but it still wasn't your fault. The man that broke your heart doesn't mean you're not worthy of being loved, and someone trying to make you feel small is because that's how they feel about themselves. Underlying issues are very real, and we

13

wouldn't spend so much time trying to clap back and get our lick back if we understood this. Someone else's insecurities are not ours; we can't let people project their hurt onto us.

I know we weren't there when Jesus asked the Father to forgive **"them,"** but that includes us! We, too, are part of "them" because we were born into sin and needed forgiveness. The next time someone hurts or offends you, remember to forgive. It may not happen overnight, but it must happen. They may never apologize but find the closure you need to move forward because forgiveness is for you. You are no longer a victim; you are victorious in Christ Jesus! Get free! Stay free!

Joy vs. Happiness

You reveal the path of life to me; in your presence is abundant joy; at your right hand are eternal pleasures. – Psalm 16:11

Happiness is an incredible feeling; however, it can come and go. Money can make you happy, but you can quickly become sad when you're broke. Friends can make you happy, but when there are disagreements and arguments, you can become upset. Being in the presence of God gives you complete joy because nothing or no one can satisfy you like He can.

I've been in the presence of others, and sometimes I've left mad and other times I left happy, but nothing else matters when I'm truly in the presence of God. I have come before the Lord disappointed and frustrated many times, but when I laid all my problems at His feet, I experienced the fullness of joy. If you need joy, check what and who's around you and remind yourself in moments of weakness that the joy of the Lord is your strength.

Not Just Healed but Made Whole

"Daughter, he said to her, your faith has saved you. Go in peace and be healed from your affliction." - Mark 5:34

The woman with the issue of blood fought her way to healing, and because of her faith, she wasn't just healed but made whole. I'm a witness that Jesus will perform surgery on your heart and make you brand new.

All sickness isn't physical but also can be emotional, spiritual, and mental. You aren't feeling well because of the lies, betrayal, character assassination, grief, divorce, loss, self-condemnation, disappointment, and rejection, but true healing is released when you acknowledge that you're sick.

We've been in a pandemic for over two years, and it was mandated that we had to wear a mask, but pre-pandemic, we were already wearing them. As women, we're good at disguising and trying to hide pain, but what you try to hide has a way of telling off on you. We pretend that we're fine but deep down there is so much pain, and trauma.

I heard someone say that the wound wasn't your fault, but your healing is your responsibility. Healing requires work and if we don't do our part, we won't get well. That's like having health insurance to go see about yourself but not going because you just don't feel like it. The woman with the issue of blood was tired of being sick and tired, and when it gets to that point, you will do ANYTHING necessary to get relief. She didn't care about being judged or embarrassed. She just wanted Jesus. Being sick that long with that kind of issue, I'm sure she began to smell. Your sickness has a smell. Anger, bitterness, gossip, jealousy, and pride have a foul odor and must be dealt with from the root.

I'm praying for you sister, that you press your way through the crowd to have a personal encounter with Jesus. All you need is one touch.

Can't Do it Without Love

By this everyone will know that you are my disciples, if you love one another - John 13:35

The Bible talks about how wickedness will increase more because love for humanity will grow cold. You've been betrayed by someone who claimed to love you, but your heart is still beating, which tells me you have a lot of love to give.

People won't know that we're children of God by our social status, how much money we have, or by how popular we are, but they will be able to identify us by our love. We cannot confess to having a relationship with God but don't have love for one another. The enemy isn't after our stuff; he's after our **joy**. Satan doesn't want us to walk in **peace** or to have true **love** in our hearts.

God is love, and if we're a part of Him, we must display His characteristics. He didn't suggest that we love one another; He commanded it. If you're struggling and don't know what real love is, open your heart and allow God to show you.

Peace Over Everything

**Thou wilt keep *him* in perfect
peace, *whose* mind *is* stayed *on thee*:
because he trusteth in thee. - Isaiah
26:3**

There is nothing in the world like peace!
Your social status, title, and money can't
give you peace when you're worried
about your children at night. What about
that time you had more bills than money?
Only the peace of God can calm your
spirit when the storm of life is raging.
When earthly experiences are too much
to bear, we need heaven's intervention on
how we should proceed.

I come to speak peace over your life
where there is confusion. I pray right now
for you to have precision in your
thoughts. I declare and decree that you
will think on those things that are lovely,
pure, honest, and praiseworthy. When
thoughts of doubt, fear, and negativity try
to creep up, we must wash our minds in

the Word of God. Let this mind be in you, my sister, which was also in Christ Jesus.

Trust the Process

Trust in the LORD with all your heart, and do not rely on your own understanding. - Proverbs 3:5

Without a test, there will not be a testimony! Tests and trials come to make us strong. I love what my Pastor Bryan Williams says, "Sometimes God has to teach our test a lesson." His phrase speaks volumes to me because we give the enemy too much credit. Not that Satan isn't a liar, the accuser of the brethren, or the evil one. However, God must show the fire "you can't burn my child," and He has shown the storm "you can't defeat my daughter."

Nothing catches God by surprise. His lessons are designed to teach us what we need to learn. I don't care how intellectual I am, God's revelation can reveal what I don't know. I may not always understand what He's doing, but I must trust that His plans for my life will prosper and not harm me. We beat ourselves up because we're not where we want to be, but trusting the process has us exactly where we should be.

The steps of a good man (woman) are ordered by the Lord. The grace you extend to everyone else needs to be given to you as well. Your process will not be like anyone else's so don't spend time competing or comparing. The journey God has you on is just for you.

ABOUT THE AUTHOR

Deana S. Drake is a native of Nashville, Tennessee. She attended Life Christian University (Nashville Campus), where she received her Associate's Degree in Theology.

Deana S. Drake is an active member of Church of the Messiah Nashville, TN, under the leadership of Pastor Bryan Williams Sr, where she serves as an Elder, Teacher, and Administrative Assistant. Her passion for women has led her to play an active role in mentorship and start Deana Shares, a Sisterhood for women.

Deana S. Drake is married to Simba Drake, and through their union, she gained three bonus children Kedarius, Keshawn, and Jaquai. She's also the proud (Mom-Tie) guardian of her 12-year-old niece Nia.